25¢

W9-CKK-540

WEE PAWS
IN THE KITCHEN

Wee Paws in the Kitchen,

Meals for you and your best friend.

BY SUE BERKMAN

ILLUSTRATED BY ERIC GURNEY

A Stuart L. Daniels Book

HAWTHORN BOOKS, INC.

PUBLISHERS / *New York*

To Godfrey and Adam

S. B.

To Poopsie and Cara

E. G.

CONTENTS

1

2

3

WEE PAWS
IN THE KITCHEN

CHAPTER 1

BY PUPULAR
DEMAND

When was the last time you looked into a pair of limpid brown eyes and said, "Sometimes you're almost human"? That hangdog expression you no doubt got in return was simply your dog telling you that he's not "sometimes" or "almost"—he's *always* and *totally* human. He enjoys curling up in the same overstuffed chair you enjoy curling up in; he's with you when it comes to that extra five minutes after the alarm goes off; he likes to be cool when it's hot and warm when it's cold. Most of all, he likes to eat what you like to eat—meat! The next time you attack a rare T-bone, you are sure to be shown in no uncertain terms that

1

his nose is rather out of joint over the fact that you've served him the same old dog meal *à la maison.*

The answer, of course, is compromise. Just one or two special dishes can make the difference between a ho-ho and a ho-hum diet for your dog. He'll devour these treats with glee, and chances are he'll know just when they're in the works.

They are *not* meant to replace his regular foods. On the contrary, commercially prepared products are nutritionally more complete than any combination you could possibly devise. The fact of the matter is that by serving him an occasional made-by-hand meal, he will probably come to look upon his packaged rations with renewed interest or at least with a minimum of disdain.

Most of the dishes presented here yield two servings, one for you and one for your dog. If the family of dogs or humans is larger, double or triple the recipe ingredients. Try a new recipe on each quiet evening when you and yours are dining in solitude. Make a big fuss; do it up big. He'll love it, and you'll love watching him love it. Don't be surprised if you discover that you, too, look forward to these special times with eager anticipation. After all, that's the way the biscuit breaks.

Be Anything But Dogmatic

Be prepared for your dog to turn up his nose at an old-favorite food, to eat less on some days than others, to feel somewhat unsettled for no apparent reason. Even though *you* may go "according to the book," remember that you dog has not read it. When he takes issue, just make it your business to turn over a new leaf. Once you've made sure that the food is not too hot for him to handle, remember that a missed meal never hurt any dog, and by showing worry or displeasure or trying to tempt him with a fingerful from the dish, you may succeed only in establishing a pattern that will make him a finicky eater for the rest of his life.

By the time your dog reaches maturity, his food intake may be adjusted to one meal a day. Most experts advise an evening feeding to make it easier for your dog to settle comfortably for the night, but if it is more convenient for you to establish a regular morning routine, by all means do so. On the other hand, you may find that the best solution is a twice-a-day feeding, which allows him half of his daily ration at each meal.

Wagging the Old Wives' Tales

Here are the facts about old notions to help set your thinking straight.

Worms do not come from raw meat or milk. Worms come from worm eggs, and these are not found in government-inspected milk or meat. Freshly killed animals may contain tapeworm and therefore should not be eaten. Pork, of course, should always be cooked to avoid trichinosis. Remember, too, that a diet consisting solely of meat (raw or cooked) will be lacking in certain essential nutrients, and the signs of these deficiencies will soon begin to show.

Eczema is not caused by starchy foods. Starch, a necessary part of your dog's diet, is easily digested if well cooked and does not cause eczema.

Bones are not necessary for developing strong teeth. Your dog may enjoy them, however, and if you have a heavy knucklebone, by all means let him have a go at it. Take care

to keep him from sharp bones from chops, poultry, or fish, which may splinter and cause serious intestinal damage.

Grass is not a tonic. Grass provides nothing in the way of nutrients that your dog can't get from a regular balanced diet. Indeed, grass may cause intestinal trouble.

Garlic is not a good worm remedy. Garlic and raw onions will serve only to bring on a second set of problems, like intestinal upset and indigestion. Consult your veterinarian for a good worm medicine.

After Every Meal . . .

After he's finished his meal, you may spot your dog heading for the nearest carpet, where he will rub both sides of his face several times. That's his "big napkin on the floor," so unless it's a priceless Persian, just ignore this little part of his personal toilette.

His teeth, too, need a certain amount of care to keep

tartar from accumulating in excess. Pick up a package of dried-beef rawhide in the pet store or supermarket, and offer him one as a kind of after-dinner mint.

Eating with Relish

Some dogs will lick the platter clean so fast that you'll wonder if you've served enough. Don't worry. Most dogs don't know the meaning of self-feeding and will eat as much as you put into the dish. Only when he has gorged himself past capacity will he realize that he has had enough, and by then it may be too late to prevent him from losing the entire meal. Overfeeding, in the long run, will do more harm than underfeeding, so let quality rather than quantity be your guide.

Sometimes this pattern of food-bolting is set when there

is more than one dog in the household. Perhaps feeding each on opposite sides of the room will relieve their anxiety that they won't have the whole meal to themselves.

In any event, don't be concerned if your dog wolfs his food. Just sit back and be proud that you've given him something he enjoys so much.

Putting On the Dog

Company coming? Remember you're opening your dog's house, too. So why not suggest that your guests bring along

their dog to keep yours occupied and away from the dinner table. Take a little time to whip up a special treat, and set aside a corner of the room where you may lay out a couple of festive place mats and bright dishes. Just watch your pup play the proud host!

Designed for the Dog Carte

When you take to the road with your dog, be sure to take along foods that he is well used to. He is likely to consider the change in routine bad enough without having to cope with a change of diet, too. A combination of the two may bring about the accident you hope to avoid.

Bring along a supply of drinking water also, since it is not always readily available on the road. Even when it is, a water change may cause digestive upset.

When He's Sick as a You-Know-What

When your dog isn't feeling up to snuff, you'd be wise to watch his diet for a couple of days until you're sure he's back to normal.

Constipation is often normal and may be caused simply by a lack of regular exercise. Try a little milk of magnesia (1 teaspoon for each 10 pounds of body weight), but avoid other laxatives intended for humans. Do not, under any circumstances, give a laxative if you suspect that the problem is the result of a foreign object he has swallowed.

Diarrhea is not a usual cause for concern unless it is accompanied by other symptoms, such as rapid breathing, vomiting, or abdominal pain. Watch for these symptoms. In the meantime, give him a little Kaopectate (1 teaspoon per 10 pounds of body weight), limit his diet to bland foods, such as cooked rice or other starches, and avoid fluid foods, such as milk or broth.

Chances are he won't be very enthusiastic about eating at all, and at first you'd do well to comply with his wishes. The notion that nature takes care of its own is a fine one, but bear in mind that your veterinarian can help you to help nature take care of *your* own a little bit faster.

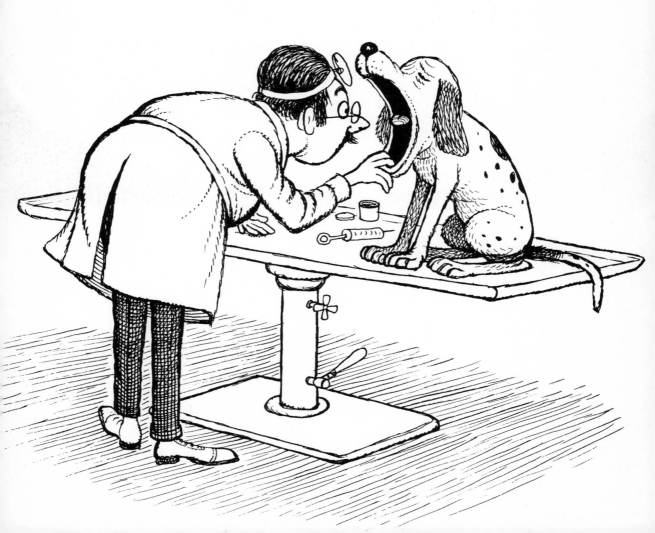

The Old Dog Tray

Dogs, like humans, deserve extra care as they get older. This means that you should recognize the fact that his nutritional needs and appetite are not what they used to be. Try to reduce the size of his meals in relation to his lessened activity. You might divide his ration into two or more small meals a day, just to provide a bit of interest. Be sure that he has access to fresh water at all times, since kidney problems are quite common, as is constipation. Above all, be sure to avoid any unnecessary change in his feeding schedule, since by now he has established a routine that is clearly his way of life.

CHAPTER 2

FEEDING ON
ALL FOURS

All living things need food for growth, energy, and tissue repair. Most animals are guided by instinct in their selection of the "right" foods, but your pet's demands can go only as far as your supply allows. Proper feeding simply means supplying daily an adequate quantity of all nutrients in the correct proportions.

Qualitatively, dogs require essentially the same nutrients as man. The following is a summary prepared by the Committee on Animal Nutrition of the National Research Council:

NUTRIENT REQUIREMENTS OF DOGS [1]
(Amounts per pound of body weight per day)

Nutrients	Weight of dog in pounds	Adult maintenance	Growing puppies
Energy (kcal) [2]	5	50.0	100.0
	10	42.0	84.0
	15	35.0	70.0
	30	32.0	64.0
	50 and over	31.0	62.0
Protein—minimum (gm)		2.0	4.0
Carbohydrate—maximum (gm)		4.6	7.2
Fat (gm)		0.6	1.2
Minerals:			
Calcium (mg)		120.000	240.000
Phosphorus (mg)		100.000	200.000
Iron (mg)		0.600	0.600
Copper (mg)		0.075	0.075
Cobalt (mg)		0.025	0.025
Sodium Chloride (mg)		170.000	240.000
Potassium (mg)		100.000	200.000
Magnesium (mg)		5.000	10.000
Manganese (mg)		0.050	0.100
Zinc (mg)		0.050	0.100
Iodine (mg)		0.015	0.030
Vitamins:			
Vitamin A (IU)		45.0000	90.0000
Vitamin D (IU)		3.0000	9.0000
Vitamin E (mg)		—[3]	1.0000
Vitamin B_{12} (mg)		0.0003	0.0006
Folic acid (mg)		0.0020	0.0040
Riboflavin (mg)		0.0200	0.0400
Pyridoxine (mg)		0.0100	0.0200
Pantothenic acid (mg)		0.0230	0.0450
Niacin (mg)		0.1100	0.1800
Choline (mg)		15.0000	30.0000

[1] Symbols: gm = gram; mg = milligram; IU = International Unit.

[2] Values listed are for gross, or calculated, energy. Biologically available energy is ordinarily 75–85 percent of the calculated.

[3] Amount not established.

Energy Calories

The solid basis for your dog's adequate diet is food energy. It must be assumed that adequate calories are supplied, for if

this is not the case, the energy deficit may cause utilization of protein and fat for energy rather than for other essential requirements. Too many calories, on the other hand, will cause obesity.

Individual dogs differ greatly in their calorie needs, even when size, activity levels, and environments are similar. Generalizations become even more impossible when factors such as body conformations, hair coat, and disposition are also taken into account. Special consideration must also be allowed in the feeding of puppies, pregnant and lactating bitches, older dogs, and sick dogs.

A large selection of excellent dog foods is available from reputable manufacturers. These foods contain all of the essential nutrients in proper proportion and are the simplest and most economical way to feed a dog correctly.

Protein

When proteins are eaten, the digestive processes of a healthy dog break them down into amino acids, which pass into the blood and are carried throughout the body. The cells select the amino acids they need and use them in constructing new body tissue and such vital substances as antibodies, hormones, enzymes, and blood cells. As in the human, a dog's body is made largely of protein—skin, muscles, internal organs, nails, hair, brain, and bones. For strong muscles, healthy hair and nails, and high energy levels, protein must be present in the dog's body at all times. Proteins are also necessary for proper digestion, for preventing body fluids from becoming too acid or alkaline, and for regulating important body processes. Good sources of protein are meats, poultry, fish, eggs, dairy products, yeast, and wheat germ.

Carbohydrates

Although it has not been established that dogs have any specific requirement for carbohydrates, they do have an important role as a source of calories. Apparently dogs can utilize large amounts of carbohydrates in properly balanced diets, but care should be taken that the diet also allows for sufficient protein, fat, and minerals. For the most satisfactory use in the dog's diet, starches should always be cooked, since a high dietary level of raw starch is likely to result in diarrhea. Good sources of carbohydrates are whole-grain bread, rice, fruits, cereals, and other grain products.

Fats

Fat is essential in the diet of a normal, healthy dog, although minimum requirements have not been established as yet. Fat-deficient dogs quickly develop dry hair and dry, scaly skin, and they appear to be more susceptible to infec-

tion than dogs whose diets contain fat in adequate supply. Fats supply essential fatty acids for a concentrated source of energy, and they also contribute to the palatability and texture of dry dog foods. Excess fat will result in caloric needs being met before sufficient food can be consumed to provide the protein, minerals, and vitamins necessary for health. Good sources of fats are natural vegetable oils and lard.

Minerals and Vitamins

Following is a list of the minerals and vitamins needed by dogs, indicating why they are needed as well as the principal source of supply.

MINERAL AND VITAMIN CHART

Mineral or vitamin	Deficiency will cause	Principal sources
Calcium	Rickets; bowed legs and other bone malformation in puppies; osteomalacia in adults; hyperirritability of muscle and nerves; reduced lactation	Whole or skim milk, yogurt
Iron	Anemia; fatigue; sometimes diarrhea	Liver, yeast, wheat germ, meats, egg yolks, whole-grain bread and cereals
Magnesium	Hyperirritability; convulsions	Whole grains, vegetables (especially green leafy ones)
Phosphorus	Essentially the same as calcium deficiency	Milk, eggs, cheese, meats
Potassium	Impaired growth; nervous restlessness; poor muscle tone; paralysis	Vegetables, meats, fish
Trace minerals (copper, cobalt,[1] manganese,[1] zinc[1]), sodium, chlorine	Poor growth; fatigue; skin disorders; impaired reproduction	Seafoods, liver, green leafy vegetables, egg yolks
Vitamin A	Growth failure in puppies; ophthalmia or eye infection leading to blindness; proneness to infections of ears, mouth, respiratory, digestive, and urogenital tracts; complete reproductive failure	Yellow fruits and vegetables, cream, butter or margarine, eggs, liver and other organ meats
Vitamin B$_{12}$	Growth failure; anemia; reproduction impairment	Milk, eggs, cheese, most muscle meats, liver
Vitamin C	Scurvy may occur in special cases; falling hair; loss of teeth; brittle bones	Formed by natural body processes in the dog
Vitamin D	Rickets; bowed legs and other bone malformations; poor teeth; loss of muscle tone; failure to assimilate calcium and phosphorus	Vitamin D enriched milk, fish liver oil

[1] Experimental proof of the precise need for these in dogs is lacking, although the need itself is recognized.

Mineral or vitamin	Deficiency will cause	Principal sources
Vitamin E	Impairment of growth; breeding failure; muscle degeneration; abnormal lactation	Wheat germ, unrefined vegetable oil
Vitamin K	Failure of blood to clot properly	Dogs are able to synthesize Vitamin K in the digestive tract
Choline	Growth failure in puppies; fatty livers and cirrhosis	Brains, liver, yeast, wheat germ, kidney, egg yolks
Folic acid	Loss of appetite and growth failure in puppies; reduced antibody production	Liver, green vegetables
Niacin	Black tongue, a disease similar to pellagra in man; nervous disorders; appetite loss and emaciation	Yeast, liver, wheat germ, kidney, fish, muscle meats, eggs
Pantothenic acid	Erratic appetite; growth failure; collapse; convulsions; coma in acute deficiency	Liver, kidney, heart, yeast, wheat germ, whole-grain bread and cereal, green vegetables
Pyridoxine	Anemia; nerve degeneration; loss of appetite; growth failure; emaciation	Yeast, wheat germ, liver, heart, kidney
Riboflavin (B$_2$)	Growth failure in puppies; weakness; diarrhea; watery bloodshot eyes; collapse and death in acute deficiency	Liver, yeast, milk, cooked leafy vegetables
Thiamine (B$_1$)	Loss of appetite; failure to grow; nervous disorders; paralysis; impaired gastric secretion	Brewers' yeast, wheat germ, rice polish, pork, kidney, heart

The recipes in this book have been constructed with your pet's nutritional needs in mind. Remember, these are treats for your faithful friend and should be presented only occasionally as a supplement to his regular meals of commercial dog food. These dishes are not the same as feeding your animal scraps of leftovers, which are often given with no consideration of their nutritional content.

CHAPTER 3

ANIMAL FARE

THE BIG GRIND

Ground beef is a great basic food for your dog's diet. It may be prepared in any number of ways. The simplest and perhaps best method (since none of the valuable nutrients is lost in cooking) is to place the allotted amount of beef in a bowl, add a small amount of boiling water, and set aside to cool. This will remove the blood redness from the meat and still leave a tasty juice, which your dog will surely enjoy.

Ground beef may also be shaped into patties and broiled or sautéed in a heavy skillet. Before cooking you may mix a raw egg into the meat or even bits of diced vegetables, which have been left over from your family's meal.

Ground beef is a dependable source of protein. For even more nutrition combine the beef mixture with ground liver or other organ meat, and your dog will have a terrific supply of iron and vitamin A.

CHOW-CHOW CHOW MEIN

This dish will provide your dog with a good supply of protein, minerals, and vitamins.

⅓ *pound pork tenderloin or shoulder*
Pinch of salt
⅔ *tablespoon shortening*
⅓ *cup finely chopped celery*
⅙ *cup thinly sliced canned or fresh mushrooms*
⅓ *can bean sprouts or Chinese vegetables, drained*
⅔ *cup water or meat broth*
⅓ *tablespoon flour*
⅓ *tablespoon water*
⅓ *tablespoon sugar*
Cooked noodles or rice (optional)

Cut pork into thin strips, and season with salt; brown in a little of the shortening in a heavy skillet. Add to the skillet the remaining shortening and the celery, mushrooms, and bean sprouts. Cook, stirring, until vegetables are golden brown. Add water or meat broth, and simmer for 20 to 30 minutes. Blend flour with water, and slowly stir roux into vegetable mixture. Cook 10 minutes. Add sugar. May be served with cooked noodles or rice.

Makes 2 servings.

PURE BRED PUDDING

Try putting a little pudding in his dish for calcium and carbohydrate.

¾ cup toasted bread cubes
1 egg
1 cup milk
1 cup sugar
Pinch of salt
1 tablespoon melted butter or margarine

Preheat oven to 350°. Place bread cubes in a small casserole. Beat the egg until foamy. Scald the milk, and gradually beat into the egg; beat in sugar, salt, and butter. Pour milk mixture over bread cubes, and bake for 25 minutes.

Makes 2 servings.

BEAGLE BAGELS

Here is a treat with benefits: carbohydrate, Vitamin A, and other vitamins and minerals.

1 bagel, plain, egg, or whole wheat
2 tablespoons cream cheese, softened

Place bagel in preheated oven until just warm. Spread with softened cream cheese. Cut into bite-sized pieces, and serve.

Makes 1 serving.

BORZOI BORSCH

Beets are an excellent source of vitamins and minerals.

1 No. 1 can shredded beets, with liquid
2 cups beef bouillon
3 tablespoons lemon juice
¼ teaspoon salt
Sour cream or yogurt (optional)

Combine beets and liquid with bouillon in a saucepan. Bring to a boil, and simmer for 10 to 20 minutes. Add lemon juice and salt. Serve warm or cold with a tablespoon of sour cream or yogurt if your dog enjoys it.

Makes 3 servings.

DACHSHUND LOX

1 bagel
2 tablespoons cream cheese, softened
1 piece Nova Scotia salmon

Prepare bagel as in Beagle Bagels (page 27). Spread with softened cream cheese, and top with Nova Scotia salmon. Cut into bite-sized pieces, and serve.

Makes 1 serving.

TERRIERYAKI

Good taste *and* good protein are combined in this one.

> *1 pound fillet of beef or any very tender cut of boneless*
>   *steak*
> *¼ cup soy sauce*
> *¾ tablespoon sugar*

Cut beef into slices ¼ inch thick. Place slices between sheets of waxed paper, and pound lightly with a mallet or the flat side of a large kitchen knife. Combine soy sauce and sugar; pour over meat, and let marinate 1 hour, turning slices occasionally. Broil beef slices about 1 minute on each side, placing meat 2 to 3 inches from source of heat. Cut into small pieces, and serve.

Makes about 3 servings.

PULI PUPRIKASH

Fowl is always fair game for protein, minerals, and vita-mins—especially vitamin A.

1 chicken breast, split and boned
1 tablespoon shortening
⅓ 10½-ounce can condensed tomato soup
⅛ cup sour cream
⅓ cup sliced mushrooms, drained
Cooked noodles (optional)

In a heavy skillet brown the chicken in shortening; pour off fat, and add the tomato soup, sour cream, and mush-rooms. Cover; cook over low heat for about 45 minutes or until chicken is tender. May be served over cooked noodles if desired.
Makes 2 servings.

MAD DOG MILK SHAKE

A milk shake is rich in calories—protein, calcium, phosphorus, and vitamin A, too.

1 cup milk
½ cup ice cream (any flavor)

Combine milk and ice cream in blender. Blend 1 minute. Pour into soup dish, and serve.
Makes 1 serving.

HARE OF THE DOG

1 small rabbit (about 1 pound)
Salt
Flour for dredging
1 tablespoon butter
1 tablespoon shortening
1 tablespoon flour
¾ to 1 cup top milk or thin cream

Rinse the rabbit, dry, and cut into small serving pieces; sprinkle with salt, and dredge in flour. Heat butter and shortening in a heavy skillet. Brown rabbit pieces quickly on all sides. Reduce heat, and simmer very slowly about 1 hour. Remove rabbit from skillet, and drain off all but 1 tablespoon fat and drippings. Blend 1 tablespoon flour into remaining fat and drippings, and brown. Add milk, and simmer until mixture thickens. Pour over rabbit, and serve.
Makes 2 servings.

HARE OF THE DOG #2

1 very small rabbit
1 cup water
½ teaspoon salt
1 sprig parsley
½ stalk celery, diced
2 tablespoons butter or margarine
2 tablespoons flour
½ cup milk
1 cup whole kernel corn, drained
1 cup whole tomatoes, drained

Soak rabbit in salted water for ½ hour; drain. Put into a large heavy kettle or a Dutch oven with 1 cup water, ½ teaspoon salt, parsley, and celery; bring to a boil. Cover; simmer for 1½ hours or until very tender. Preheat oven to 350°. In a small saucepan melt butter, and stir in flour. Transfer rabbit into a 2½-quart casserole. Strain and reserve ½ cup of the liquid; stir slowly into butter and flour. Add milk. Cook, stirring, until thick and boiling. Add corn and tomatoes. Pour mixture over rabbit in the casserole. Cover and bake about 30 minutes or until hot and bubbly.

Makes 2 servings.

SPRINGER SOUP

Springer Soup provides a big bowl of Vitamin A along with essential minerals.

> ½ head bibb or Boston lettuce
> 1 cup coarsely chopped spinach
> 1 stalk celery, diced
> ¾ quart chicken stock
> 1 tablespoon butter or margarine
> Sour cream (optional)

Tear lettuce leaves into small pieces, and combine with spinach in a large saucepan. Add the celery, stock, and butter or margarine. Cook over medium heat for 30 minutes, stirring occasionally. Remove from heat, and spoon into a bowl. Top with a tablespoon of sour cream if desired.

Makes 1 serving.

GERMAN SHEPHERD PIE

> 1 pound ground beef
> Pinch of salt
> 1 package brown-gravy mix (yield of 1 cup)
> 1 cup water
> 1 10-ounce package frozen peas and carrots
> ¼ cup packaged shredded cheddar cheese
> 1½ cups warm mashed potatoes

Preheat oven to 450°. Cook ground beef in a skillet over moderately high heat until meat is browned. Add a pinch of salt; blend in gravy mix and water, stirring until thick-ened. Add vegetables; cover and simmer for 5 minutes. Pour into casserole. Fold cheese into mashed potatoes; spoon over meat mixture. Bake for 15 minutes or until potatoes are lightly browned.

Makes 4 servings.

YORKSHIRE PUDDING

This dish accompanies the family roast-beef dinner. Doggie will appreciate some of the pudding with his share.

> *1 egg*
> *5 tablespoons sifted flour*
> *Pinch of salt*
> *1 cup milk*
> *6 tablespoons hot beef drippings*

Thoroughly beat the egg; add 2 tablespoons of the flour, and mix well. Add remaining 3 tablespoons of flour and the salt, mixing well. Add the milk; combine mixture thor-oughly, using an eggbeater. Pour the beef drippings into a deep casserole, and place in oven until the drippings are sizzling hot. Beat pudding mixture again, and pour into the sizzling drippings. Place in oven, along with the family roast, and cook about 50 minutes or until top is crisp and browned.

Makes 1 serving.

HUSH PUPPIES

There are many variations on the theme of how hush puppies originated, but the most popular version seems to center around an old Southern plantation kitchen where hungry, yapping dogs were annoying a busy cook. Throwing a few spoonfuls of prepared corn-bread batter into deep fat, she tossed the golden-brown cooked puffs to the dogs with the command "Hush, puppies."

1 cup white cornmeal
½ cup sweet milk
2 tablespoons vegetable oil or shortening
¼ teaspoon salt
1 egg, well beaten
Fat

Combine all ingredients, and mix well. Drop by table-spoonfuls into deep, hot fat, and fry until golden brown.

For baked version, preheat oven to 400°. Prepare batter as above, but use less milk. Drop by spoonfuls onto greased cookie sheet, and bake until golden brown.

Makes 1 dozen.

HOT DOG BITES

¾ pound cocktail frankfurters
Butter, margarine, or vegetable oil

Rub frankfurters with butter, margarine, or oil. Broil 3 inches from heat, turning with tongs to brown evenly.
Makes 2 servings.

POOCHED SALMON

3 cups beef or vegetable bouillon
Small piece of salmon, boned and dressed

Heat bouillon to boiling, and reduce heat so that liquid continues to simmer. Wrap salmon in cheesecloth, and gently lower into liquid. Cover; simmer for 30 to 40 minutes or until fish flakes easily. Cool slightly before serving.
Makes 1 serving.

PUPPYETTES DE VEAU

2 thin slices of veal
1 tablespoon butter or margarine, melted
½ cup mushrooms, sliced or chopped

Brush one side of each veal slice with melted butter or margarine. Spread mushrooms evenly on buttered side of meat; roll up, and secure with toothpick. Arrange in a buttered heavy skillet, and braise over low to medium heat until meat is fork-tender.
Makes 2 servings.

KIDNEYS K-NINE

2 veal kidneys
¼ pound mushrooms, sliced
2 tablespoons butter or margarine
¼ cup heavy cream
Pinch of salt
Buttered toast (optional)

Remove hard core and excess fat from kidneys; cut into thin slices. Sauté slices and mushrooms in butter or margarine in a large skillet for about 5 minutes or until lightly browned. Add cream and salt, and heat thoroughly. Serve over bite-sized pieces of buttered toast if desired.

Makes 2 servings.

BULLDOG DRUMSTICKS

3 tablespoons soy sauce
3 tablespoons lemon juice
⅛ teaspoon onion powder
2 chicken or turkey legs
1 tablespoon honey
1 tablespoon catsup
Salt

Mix soy sauce, lemon juice, and onion powder; pour over chicken or turkey legs in a deep bowl. Cover loosely, and marinate in refrigerator for several hours. When ready to

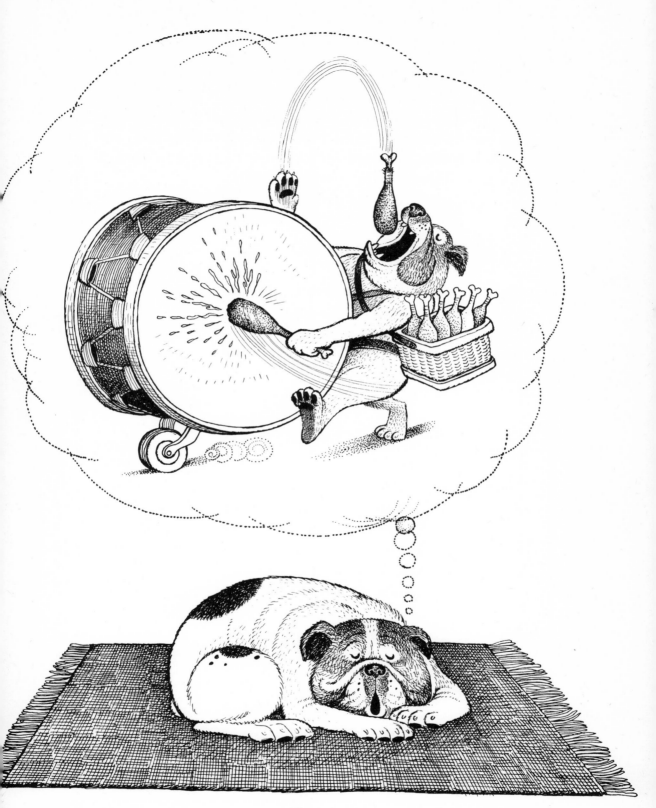

cook, arrange legs on foil-lined broiler pan. Mix together the honey, catsup, and 1 tablespoon of the marinade; brush half of the baste on the legs. Sprinkle with salt, and broil about 25 minutes. Turn; brush with remaining baste, and broil another 25 minutes or until meat is tender. Remove all bones before serving.

Makes 2 servings.

COLLIE FLOUR BISCUITS

2 cups sifted all-purpose flour
1½ teaspoons baking powder
½ teaspoon salt
⅙ cup shortening
⅜ cup milk

Preheat oven to 425°. Sift flour, baking powder, and salt together into a mixing bowl. Cut in shortening with pastry blender until mixture resembles coarse cornmeal. Add milk, mixing lightly until dough holds together. Transfer dough to floured board. Knead lightly; roll dough ½ inch thick; cut into rounds or other shapes with floured cutter. Bake on lightly greased cookie sheet for 12 to 15 minutes, until lightly browned. Serve at once with a pat of butter.

Makes 8 biscuits.

FLOUR

WESTPORT FLOUR CO. LTD

47

PLAIN PUPOVERS

⅓ cup flour, sifted
⅙ teaspoon salt
1 small egg, lightly beaten
⅓ cup milk
Butter

Preheat oven to 450°. Sift flour together with salt. Combine lightly beaten egg with the milk, and mix with dry ingredients. Heat a muffin pan till very hot, and butter well. Fill cups halfway with batter. Bake at 450° for 20 minutes; reduce heat to 375°, and bake for another 20 to 30 minutes, or until popovers are browned and firm.

Makes 3 popovers.

GREAT DANISH PASTRY

1 package refrigerated crescent dinner rolls
1 egg, beaten
1 tablespoon granulated sugar
1 cup confectioners' sugar
1 tablespoon softened butter or margarine
4 teaspoons milk

Preheat oven to 375°. Shape crescent dinner rolls into 2 large rectangular pieces, and cut each rectangle into 3 strips. Twist two strips together into the shape of a rope, pinch the ends, and arrange the strip on a greased cookie sheet in the shape of an S. Bring ends to center to form a figure 8. Repeat with remaining strips. Brush each with the beaten egg, and sprinkle with granulated sugar. Bake 10 to 12 minutes or until golden brown. While pastries are baking, prepare icing by combining confectioners' sugar, butter, and milk in a small bowl; blend well. When pastries are done, remove from oven, and immediately drizzle icing over each. Serve warm.

Makes 3 pastries.

POODLE STRUDEL

2 cups unsifted all-purpose flour
1½ teaspoons baking powder
¼ teaspoon salt
⅜ cup sugar
¼ cup vegetable oil
1 tablespoon butter or margarine, melted
1 tablespoon orange juice
2 eggs
½ cup soft white raisins
1 teaspoon cinnamon
2 teaspoons sugar
1 egg white, slightly beaten

Preheat oven to 350°. Sift flour, baking powder, salt, and ⅜ cup sugar into a bowl. Make a well in the center, and add oil, butter, orange juice, and eggs; mix to form a soft dough. Knead on a floured board until the dough is smooth. Separate evenly into 2 pieces. Roll each piece out to form a circle about ¼ inch thick; spread with raisins. Mix cinnamon with 2 teaspoons of sugar, and sprinkle lightly over raisins. Roll tightly, and place on a greased cookie sheet. Prick the top with a fork, brush with egg white, and sprinkle with remaining cinnamon-sugar mixture. Bake for about 45 minutes or until golden brown. Cool, and cut into slices. Rolls may be baked and cooled, then wrapped in foil and frozen until ready to reheat and serve.

Makes 2 rolls.

BOSTON BULL SHOTS

2 beef bouillon cubes
2 cups tomato juice
2 tablespoons chopped parsley (optional)
2 lemon wedges (optional)

Heat bouillon cubes and tomato juice until cubes are dissolved. Sprinkle with chopped parsley, and serve with lemon wedges if desired. Before toasting each other's health, you may wish to flavor yours with something more spirited. Your dog will take his unflavored.

Makes 2 servings.

SCHNAUZER SCHNITZEL

1 egg
Four
Salt
Fine, dry bread crumbs
Peanut or olive oil
¾ pound veal scallops
2 sprigs parsley
2 lemon wedges

Beat egg lightly in a small bowl. Season flour with salt, and put into a separate bowl. Put bread crumbs into another bowl. Heat about 2 inches of oil in a deep, heavy skillet.

When oil is bubbly, dip each scallop in flour, then in beaten egg, and finally in bread crumbs. Fry quickly in the hot oil until golden brown on both sides. Arrange on a platter, and garnish with parsley and lemon wedges.

Makes 2 servings.

IRISH SETTER STEW

2 pounds lean shoulder of lamb, cut into serving-size
    pieces
2 medium potatoes, peeled and sliced
Salt
1 leek, sliced (white part, washed thoroughly)
1 stalk celery, cut into 3 or 4 pieces
2 sprigs parsley
1 bay leaf
1 teaspoon thyme
Water

Preheat oven to 350°. In a large casserole arrange a layer of lamb, top with a layer of potatoes, and season with salt. Repeat until all the meat and potatoes are used, ending with a layer of meat on top. Add the remaining ingredients and just enough water to cover. Cover casserole, and bake for about 1½ hours or until meat is tender. Remove bay leaf.

Makes 4 servings.

WOOF RAISERS

½ pound ground beef
¼ pound Swiss cheese, cut into strips
½ cup cooked-ham strips
1 egg, beaten
⅛ teaspoon salt
1 sprig parsley, minced

Combine all ingredients, and mix thoroughly. Shape into patties, and brown on both sides in a heavy skillet to desired doneness.

Makes 2 servings.

SEALYHAM BURGER

1 pound ground beef
2 tablespoons sour cream
1 tablespoon black caviar (optional)

Mix ingredients, and shape into two meat patties. Broil or panbroil to desired doneness.

Makes 2 servings.

COCKER-LEEKIE SOUP

6 leeks
3 cups boiling water
1½ teaspoons salt
2 tablespoons chicken fat or butter.
1½ cups well-seasoned chicken broth
½ cup light cream

Remove and discard roots and dark-green part of tops from the leeks. Wash carefully; cut in half lengthwise, then crosswise in ⅛-inch slices. Place in a pan with boiling water and salt. Simmer 5 to 7 minutes or until tender but not mushy. Add chicken fat or butter and chicken broth; heat to a boil. Scald cream, and stir into soup.

Makes 2 servings.

DALMATIAN RATION

1 10-ounce package frozen peas and carrots
1 can condensed cream of chicken soup
¾ teaspoon poultry seasoning
1 pound chicken livers
2 tablespoons butter or margarine
Salt

Cook peas and carrots as directed on package label. Drain. Add soup and poultry seasoning; heat gently. Meanwhile, sauté chicken livers in butter until thoroughly cooked. Stir in the vegetable and soup mixture, and heat gently. Season with salt to taste (your pet will probably prefer light seasoning).

Makes 4 servings.

BOXER PUNCH

⅓ *cup sugar*
2 eggs, separated
¼ *teaspoon salt*
4 cups milk, scalded
1 teaspoon vanilla
3 tablespoons sugar
Whipped cream (optional)
Nutmeg (optional)

Beat ⅓ cup sugar into 2 egg yolks in upper part of double boiler; add salt. Stir milk in slowly. Stirring constantly, cook over hot but not boiling water until mixture coats the spoon. Let cool, then add vanilla. Beat egg whites until foamy; gradually add 3 tablespoons of sugar and continue beating until soft peaks form. Fold into the custard, and mix thoroughly. Cover and chill in refrigerator 3 to 4 hours before serving. Unless you're watching your dog's weight, you might dot the top of the punch with whipped cream and a light sprinkling of nutmeg before serving.

Makes 2 servings.

BLOODHOUND PUDDING

¾ cup finely chopped onion
2 tablespoons lard
1 pound fresh pork fat, diced into ½-inch cubes
⅓ cup whipping cream
2 eggs, beaten
⅛ teaspoon thyme
½ bay leaf, pulverized
2 cups fresh pork blood
2 sausage casings

Put a large pot of water on to boil. In a large skillet sauté onions in lard until golden. Add pork fat; cook until half melted. Cool slightly, then mix in the cream, eggs, thyme, and bay leaf. Combine gently with pork blood. Fill sausage casings about ⁴⁄₅ full with mixture; seal and put into wire basket. Plunge basket into boiling water, and reduce heat to a simmer. Simmer about 20 minutes. (If any of the sausages rise to the top of the water, pierce the skins carefully to release the air.) To serve, split and grill gently. If fresh pork blood is not easily obtainable, use commercially prepared blood pudding, which comes in sausage form. All you'll have to do is split and grill.

Makes 2 servings.

DOBERMAN DUMPLINGS

1 cup ground cornmeal
1 cup pancake flour
½ teaspoon salt
1 teaspoon sugar
Cold water
2 cups beef bouillon

Combine all ingredients, except bouillon, using only enough cold water so that mixture can be molded in your hands. Pat into flat round cakes about 2 inches in diameter and ½ inch thick. Heat bouillon to boiling, and reduce to a simmer. Drop in dumplings; cover and simmer for 20 minutes. Serve dumplings and warm broth in a deep bowl.

Makes 2 servings.

MALAMUTE MEAT LOAF

¾ *pound ground beef*
¾ *cup dry bread crumbs*
⅓ *cup diced, processed American cheese*
¼ *green pepper, diced*
1 teaspoon salt
1 small bay leaf, crumbled
¼ *teaspoon thyme*
1 egg, slightly beaten
½ *10½-ounce can tomato sauce*
Butter

Preheat oven to 350°. Mix beef, crumbs, cheese, green pepper, salt, bay leaf, and thyme. Combine egg and tomato sauce; mix into meat combination. Shape into a loaf, and place in a buttered baking dish. Bake for about 1 hour or until browned and thoroughly done.

Makes 4 servings.

WEIMARANER WEINERS

4 frankfurters
¼ cup processed cheese spread
4 slices bacon

Split frankfurters open lengthwise, but do not cut all the way through. Fill split with cheese spread, and wind a bacon slice around each frankfurter; secure with a toothpick. Broil about 6 minutes, turning once, until bacon is brown and crisp. Remove the toothpicks before serving. If your Weimaraner likes peanut butter, you can substitute it for the cheese.

Makes 2 servings.

SALUKI SALAD

1 ¼ cups cooked, cold chicken cubes
¼ cup finely chopped celery
¼ cup finely chopped carrots
Mayonnaise to taste
2 tablespoons chopped parsley

Be sure you have removed all gristle, fat, skin, and bones from chicken cubes. Combine chicken with celery and carrots. Blend with mayonnaise to taste, and garnish with parsley.

Makes 2 servings.

CHIHUAHUA CHOWDER

Meat Version

5 cups beef bouillon
1 cup tomato juice
1 pound ground beef
¼ cup uncooked rice
1 egg

Combine bouillon and tomato juice in a pot; heat slowly. Mix together beef, rice, and egg; shape into small balls. Drop meatballs into bouillon mixture when liquid begins to boil. Cover and simmer for 30 minutes.

Makes 6 servings.

Fish Version

2 tablespoons butter or margarine
1 medium potato, pared and chopped
1 18-ounce can tomato juice
1 1-pound package frozen cod, haddock, or flounder
    fillets, cut into small pieces
Pinch of salt

Melt butter in a 2-quart saucepan; add potato, and cook for 10 minutes, stirring occasionally. Add tomato juice; bring to a boil. Add fish pieces. Bring to a boil again, and simmer 10 minutes or until fish flakes easily. Stir in salt. Cool before serving.

Makes 6 servings.

Vegetable Version

1 medium potato, pared and diced
1 cup water
3 slices bacon, cut into ½-inch pieces
1 cup corn kernels, with liquid
1 cup milk
Pinch of salt

Boil potato in water until thoroughly cooked. Meanwhile, fry bacon in a heavy skillet until crisp. Combine bacon, corn, milk, and salt with potato and liquid; heat. Cool slightly before serving.

Makes 2 servings.

CAIRN CORN BREAD

1 cup sifted all-purpose flour
¾ cup yellow cornmeal
1 teaspoon salt
3 teaspoons baking powder
2 eggs
1 cup milk
2 teaspoons sugar
4 tablespoons shortening

Preheat oven to 400°. Grease a 9-inch-square pan. Sift flour, cornmeal, salt, and baking powder together into a mixing bowl. Combine eggs, milk, sugar, and shortening in blender, and blend about 15 seconds or until smooth. Pour mixture over dry ingredients; stir lightly, just enough to combine the mixtures. Bake about 20 to 25 minutes or until crisp and browned.

Makes 9 squares.

MUTT'S MUTTON

2 mutton chops, about 3 inches thick
Lemon juice

Preheat oven to 400°. Roast chops in a roasting pan for about 20 minutes. Pour a small amount of lemon juice into the pan; baste chops with lemon juice and drippings. At end of cooking time put pan with chops under the broiler, and brown on both sides.

Makes 2 servings.

MALTESE MALTEDS

2 cups fresh milk
2½ tablespoons malted milk
1½ teaspoons debittered brewers' yeast
2 teaspoons sugar
¾ cup powdered milk
½ teaspoon vanilla

Combine all ingredients; shake or beat until smooth.
Makes 2 servings.

WELSH CORGI RAREBIT

2 tablespoons butter or margarine
2 tablespoons sifted flour
¼ teaspoon salt
½ 10-ounce can V-8 vegetable juice
¼ pound processed American cheese, grated
Crackers, toast, or English muffins

Melt butter or margarine in a skillet or chafing dish; stir
in flour until mixture is smooth. Add salt; stir. Mix in vegetable juice gradually. Bring to a boil, stirring continually.
Cook 2 minutes. Add cheese, and stir until melted. Serve on
crackers, toast, or toasted English muffins.
Makes 2 servings.

PEKINGESE DUCK

1 small duckling, halved or quartered
1 egg yolk
2 teaspoons soy sauce
2 tablespoons honey
1 orange, peeled and sliced (optional)
1 teaspoon butter (optional)
¼ teaspoon sesame seed (optional)

Have butcher halve or quarter the bird. When ready to cook, beat egg yolk with soy sauce and honey; brush onto all sides of duck quarters. Broil, cut side down, for 45 minutes to 1 hour. Add a little of the marinade from time to time. Move duck closer to flame toward end of cooking time so that pieces may brown and become crisp. If desired, top with peeled orange slices sautéed in butter and sesame seed. Be sure to remove all the bones before serving to your dog.

Makes 2 servings.

ROVER'S DOVER SOLE

2 ¾-pound sole fillets
½ cup light cream
1½ tablespoons flour
½ teaspoon salt
1 tablespoon olive oil
3 tablespoons butter
Juice of ½ lemon

Dip fillets in slightly salted water; drain, and wipe dry on paper towel. Pour cream into a deep plate. In a separate dish mix together flour and salt. Dip fillets in cream, then in salted flour. Sauté in olive oil until brown on one side; turn fish carefully, and brown on other side. Melt butter in a small saucepan, mix in lemon juice, and pour over fish on a platter.

Makes 2 servings.

SHIH-TZU SHISH KEBAB

2 pounds lean leg or shoulder of lamb
Olive oil
Lemon juice
Salt

Have butcher cut the meat into 1½–2-inch cubes. Arrange cubes on skewers; brush with olive oil and lemon juice, and sprinkle with salt. Broil, turning often to brown evenly, until crusty brown on the outside and pink on the inside. Remove skewer before serving to your pet. You might want to try this with Kuvasz Kasha (see page 75).

Makes 2 servings.

SCHIPPERKE SHRIMP

1 slice lemon
3 sprigs parsley
1 onion
1 teaspoon salt
1 pound shrimp, shelled and deveined

Combine lemon, parsley, onion, and salt in a kettle, and bring to a boil. Add shrimp, bring to a boil again, and simmer until shrimp turn pink. Shrimp cook in 3 to 5 minutes, depending on their size.

Makes 2 servings.

SCOTTY SCALLOPS

2 tablespoons butter or margarine
½ teaspoon minced onion
¼ teaspoon salt
½ pint small fresh scallops or ½ package defrosted
    quick-frozen scallops

Preheat broiler to 350°. Grease a shallow baking pan. Combine butter or margarine, onion, and salt. Place scallops into the pan, and brush with ½ of the butter mixture. Broil for about 4 minutes, until lightly browned. Turn scallops; brush with remaining butter mixture. Broil 5 to 6 minutes longer.

Makes 2 servings.

HUSKY MUSH

4 cups fresh milk
1 cup whole-grain cereal
1 teaspoon salt

Combine ingredients in a pan, and simmer, covered, until cereal is tender. Cook *5 minutes* if using wheat germ, ground wheat, soy grits, or quick-cooking rolled oats. Cook *10 minutes* if using untreated rolled oats or coarsely ground cereals. Cook *15 minutes* if using whole buckwheat or steel cut oats.
Makes 2 servings.

KUVASZ KASHA

1 cup kasha (buckwheat groats)
1 egg
2 cups stock or broth
Salt
4 tablespoons butter

Preheat a heavy skillet. Add kasha, and stir in egg. Continue cooking and stirring until thoroughly blended and cooked dry; add stock or broth and salt to taste. Cover tightly. Lower heat, and simmer very gently for approximately ½ hour or until groats are cooked and broth is absorbed. Mix with butter.
Makes 2 servings.

PUG CHOPS

Contrary to popular belief, there is nothing wrong with an occasional serving of pork for your pet *if it is thoroughly cooked*. To kill trichinae that may be lurking in the meat, the temperature on a meat thermometer must reach 160°. After the meat is removed from the oven, let it stand for a few minutes so that it will continue to cook with its own heat.

2 loin pork chops
½ lemon, peeled and cut into 2 slices
¼ cup bread crumbs
¾ teaspoon salt
Drippings or margarine
Juice of 1 lemon

Preheat oven to 400°. Place chops in a greased baking pan; top each with a slice of lemon, and sprinkle with crumbs and salt. Dot with drippings or margarine. Add a squeeze of lemon juice to each chop. Bake for 30 minutes or until well done.

Makes 2 servings.

KERRY BLUE CHEESE OMELET

4 eggs
4 teaspoons water or milk
½ teaspoon salt
2 tablespoons butter
Blue cheese, crumbled

Break eggs into a bowl; add milk or water and salt. Beat lightly. Melt butter in a heavy skillet until it is bubbly hot but not brown. Pour in egg mixture, and immediately begin loosening edges of mixture with a spatula, lifting eggs where they have set, to allow uncooked parts to run underneath. Sprinkle top of omelet with crumbled blue cheese a minute before it is done. Fold cheese into the center of omelet as you roll it onto a plate. Cut into small pieces, and serve.

Makes 1 serving.